MW00909853

Praise for *Chasing Memory*

"Six deceptively simple essays revolving around a Chinese-American woman's life story. . . . The spare prose and reliance on anecdote, rather than description, work well. When the author does employ analogy, it is with pleasing effect. . . . An unpretentious memoir in which less is more."

—Excerpted from *Kirkus Reviews,* April 20, 2010

"If your mother asked you to write the story of her life, would you do it? Lily Owyang took on the task after her mother's death with nothing but a few photos and scraps of memory. As she chased down the forces of love, fate, and culture that shaped her family, she created what every memoirist dreams of: an honest and absorbing self-portrait in which readers recognize pieces of themselves."

—Susan Bono, editor and author of *What Have We Here: Essays about Keeping House and Finding Home*

Chasing Memory

and Other Essays from Spaces in Between

Lily Siao Owyang

SECOND EDITION

Chasing Memory
and Other Essays from Spaces in Between

ISBN: 978-1-941066-49-2

First edition, 2010
Second edition, 2021

Book and cover design
by Jo-Anne Rosen

Cover photo: Depositphotos.com
Photo of butterfly, p. 90 © Romantiche | Dreamstime.com

Wordrunner Press
Petaluma, CA

To celebrate

Gilbert, whose presence I still feel;

our sons, Kevin, Colin;

grandsons, Ryan, David, and Connor;

my sister, Amy, sister-in-law Ruth,

nieces, Aline, Christina;

the childhood shared with my brother, George;

and, as always, Mom.

Contents

Preface to the Second Edition

Ten years have passed since the 2010 edition of *Chasing Memory and Other Essays from Spaces in Between*. In putting together this second edition, I wanted to add to the earlier stories to capture some of the experiences and rituals that reflect the passage of time. The six original essays appear with only minor adjustments. "Sparks," "Coming to Age," and "Nowadays" are new to this collection.

In 2000, we celebrated the millennium. My husband, Gilbert, turned eighty. We welcomed the birth of our grandsons, Ryan in 2000, David in 2003, and Connor in 2014. Their arrivals pushed us to move back to New England after almost two decades in California. My older grandsons, whom I wrote about in earlier essays, have grown into admirable young adults.

Gilbert died in 2018, two months before his ninety-eighth birthday. With this second edition,

I want to pass on to my grandsons additional memories about their grandfather, whom they barely got to know, and stories about family members whose blood and culture connect to them.

Chasing Memory

Thread Count

"Tell my story," my mother urged.

Over the years, I heard the request so often that I paid little attention to the rising insistence in its tone. A few months into her seventy-sixth birthday, Mom died from cervical cancer, discovered too late to mitigate the disease. The urgency of her directive two decades later, now rings fresh in my ears.

Mom was a true eccentric; she flaunted convention and changed the rules as it pleased her. She dressed in clothes she made for herself, cut her own hair, and created what my brother called "The Ruby Look." Except for the wisp of grey bangs at the forehead and on each side of her head, the hair was cut so close that she looked almost bald. A cheap barrette pinned down the long shank of grey hair she let grow in the back. She carried a pair of small scissors in her handmade bag, she said, "To clip the loose ends that stick up." Waiting at the bus stop, at a shopping mall, or riding in my car, she would feel around her head, find a stray hair, pinch it between her fingers, and with one quick clip, snip it with great delight. I used to comment about the imbalanced look the trims created for her face.

"Doesn't matter," she'd say. "The little hairs itch."

When the weather got chilly, she wore the special hat she had knitted for herself, shaped just for her head, she said.

There is much to my mother's life that I have learned, and also much more that I will never know. Mom didn't like to talk about the past, but she made it clear to me that as her eldest child, I tell her story.

"Write it down," she said. "I forget."

I tried over the years to trace the threads in my mother's life, but the high number of horizontals and verticals jumbled together in a square inch of fabric left behind a thread count inexact and often obscure.

Having entered my seventh decade, I try to retrace the more visible threads, and in the process, discover that many are woven into the nubbiness of my own life. I think back to the explanations Mom used to give about which outfit she decided to sew for me after letting me believe I had a choice in the selection. "Why bother asking me?" I would say.

"I do the sewing. I sew what I like. You can do what you want later," she said.

As I sift through the memory binder of Mom's life, events tumble out, often disconnected in sequence and chronology.

Mom was born 1912 in Nanjing (formerly Nanking), China, into a family of class and privilege. She was the eldest and only girl in a family of three children. Her life from the start was circumscribed by the expectations of culture and family.

"You did what was expected. That was the custom," she said.

My mother's father held a position in the government. His marriage to my grandmother was arranged between their two families. Mom described her family as very Western in thinking. Her parents and grandparents came from the cultural tradition of scholars and government officials that made up the higher social and educated class in China prior to the defeat of the Chinese Nationalist party in 1949 and the establishment of modern China by the Chinese Communist party.

"Grandma never had bound feet. "Mom said, "Too cruel."

The painful tradition of binding young women's feet began during the history of Imperial China between the thirteenth and nineteenth centuries and continued among many families in my grandmother's social circle, many of whom Mom described as less cultured and not urbane.

"Our family was more modern," she said. Mom was sent to college, where she completed two years before she entered into an arranged marriage to my father.

"Good match for both families. Your father was a diplomat in the Chinese Nationalist Government."

Like other privileged women in the social class of her day, Mom served as decorative appendage to her husband and bore his children.

"You were born in 1937, soon after I married your father," Mom told me, "The Japanese had invaded Nanjing. I gave you the Chinese name, *LuSan,* to commemorate the event at *Luguo Jiao,* the Marco Polo Bridge. The Japanese burned the bridge down in December, in the same year you were born."

The event, documented in history as *The Nanking Massacre,* escalated the Sino-Japanese War and hastened the outbreak of World War II. Later, Mom would change my birth date according to how she remembered the events.

"Chinese and Western calendars different," she said, "Months the same, but dates different. Good enough."

The Japanese invasion of Nanjing forced our family, along with eight others in the same diplomatic delegation, to get immediately out of the path of the advancing Japanese army and leave the city. Mom described traveling with me, an infant of only a few months, as difficult and dangerous. We escaped Nanjing to a city farther south and eventually, our journey ended up in Manila, Philippines, where my father was re-assigned and my brother, George, was born three years later in 1940.

Our family lived on a compound in Manila reserved by the Chinese Nationalist Government for diplomat families. The memories and faint glimmers I have of that time are of children my age who lived in houses around us. I was around five years old, and my brother, almost two. I remembered the serious faces and whispers of grown-ups when the news came that our fathers had been captured by the Japanese army. As official representatives of in the Chinese Nationalist Government, my father and his delegation were arrested as enemies of Japan. They were imprisoned and later executed. The documented year was 1942.

"The families couldn't leave Manila after that," Mom said. "You were children. Not your business."

I still carry an image in my mind from then of Mom opening a large brown envelope. She laid out its contents on a table, a pair of eyeglasses and a folded white handkerchief with embroidered initials. I saw Mom unfold the handkerchief, watched a lock of hair fall out.

"You remembered that?" Mom said when I asked, many years later. "The eyeglasses did not belong to your father. They belonged to another family. It was your father's handkerchief with his initials and his hair. After the Japanese executed them, everybody's belongings were just dumped into one big envelope. The families had to sort them out."

When I pushed to find out more, she said, "Everything changed because of the war. No use talking about it." This was her signal to end the conversation, and the past was put back in its place.

Mom talked often about the number of household help at her parents' home who once catered to her every wish, and the hours and days she spent playing mahjong with her friends. She maintained a lifelong passion for gambling. During the late 1960s, I used to travel from the Boston area where I was raising my family to Ventura, California, to visit Mom. She and I would make the four-hour drive from her apartment and head south to Los Angeles and the Santa Anita racetrack. Mom placed bets on horses ridden by the jockeys she followed from the *Racing Form*. When she won, we would stop for dinner along the way, and when she didn't, the ride back was long and silent.

"Nothing I can do," she'd say, "That's the odds."

I have held onto an old four-by-six inch photo of my parents, brother, and me, taken in a professional studio and printed in the warm sepia tones of old photographs. Mom said it was taken in Manila before the Japanese invasion. I look to be around four years old and my brother, one. Mom is dressed in an elegant and glamorous ivory-colored long *qipao*, the traditional Chinese dress.

Her hair is collected in an up-swept hairdo. I remember how she just stared at the photo when I first brought it to her.

"My friends say I look like Loretta Young," Mom giggled. "Long time ago."

Mom loved Hollywood movies. Her favorite actress was Loretta Young. During my visits to her in California, between trips to the racetrack, Mom and I would catch the movies at the cinema complex in Century City, Los Angeles. We would begin with a movie at 10:00 a.m. in one theater, move to the next complex for a different movie, break for lunch, and catch two more movies before making the four-hour drive back to Ventura.

In the picture, my father was dressed in a Western suit and tie. My brother was perched on a stool, dressed in a knitted two-piece outfit with Mom's hands supporting him. I wore a print dress, hair pinned away from my face, looking very serious with arms at my sides and my right forefinger pointing at the floor.

"See my long painted fingernails?" Mom said. "The *amah* (housekeeper) took care of you children. Servants did everything, cook, clean, take care of you. No more, now."

A few years after the picture was taken, my father was killed and Mom was left a widow with two young children. The time was 1942. We had to leave the Philippines. She wanted to return to her parents in China, but my grandparents were reluctant to have us do so; the country was in the midst of the war between the Nationalist and Chinese Communist troops. My grandparents urged Mom to immigrate with us to the United States.

Mom made plans. She sold her dowry, jewelry and family heirlooms in order to get the money for the voyage, but she wanted to make one last trip back to China to have her parents meet my brother, their only grandson. I was left behind under the supervision of the *amah*.

Many years later, I asked why she didn't take me along. Mom explained that my piano teacher urged her not to interrupt my lessons.

"Professor Esteban was a world famous and widely respected teacher. He believed in your talent," Mom said. "We settled in New York because he arranged a scholarship for you at the Juilliard School of Music. It was an opportunity of a lifetime."

We set sail in 1948 on the ocean liner USS United States and arrived in New York as displaced persons and refugees. I was about eleven years old, and my brother, eight. I remember seeing black and white snapshots of us on the ship, my brother and I making funny faces, looking out of portholes, and striking silly poses. *Uncle* accompanied us on the trip. Mom told us that proper to Chinese custom, *Uncle* was traveling as part of the family. My brother and I were just expected to accept *Uncle* into our lives.

I learned more details about *Uncle* and Mom's life during the years after we arrived in New York, and eventually I began to accept and appreciate the intrigue that was Mom's larger story.

Mom enrolled me at Juilliard Preparatory Division. She found a basement apartment in Lower Manhattan. We lived there for a few years, and later moved to a fifth floor walk-up in an old tenement building next to a synagogue in the immigrant Jewish section of Manhattan's Lower East Side.

Mom found a job on an assembly line in an electronics factory, making and soldering small parts for radios. She adapted her Chinese name, which meant self-determination, to the English phonetic version, "Ruby."

"My English name easier to pronounce," she said, "to get a job. "

I remember the frequent burns on her hands left by working with a hot soldering iron and heard the heavy sighs of exhaustion when she came home from work. My brother and I attended the local parochial school, and were good students. I helped Mom tend to my brother, assisted with the housework, and practiced piano every day. On Saturdays, I took the subway to Juilliard for my lessons.

"Don't make me worry," Mom used to say.

Taking the stairs to the walk-up apartment every day after school, I used to stop to sit on the steps. I looked into the windows of the synagogue next door and watched the men wrapped in their prayer shawls rock silently back and forth, intoning their prayers. I imagined the faces of the children waiting for them at home. I look back now at the young girl who used to sit there, and wish I could have extended her a loving hand of support.

Soon after we arrived in New York, Mom told my brother and me that she was pregnant with my sister. *Uncle* was not a real blood relative, she said, but was to be our stepfather. My brother and I have talked since about our recollections of that time, and a single memory holds.

"She didn't want us to know any more. She said 'not your business,'" my brother remembered.

My sister was born, fourteen years after me. Years later, I would learn from my sister that Mom shared with her many details of the past which I never knew. I realized as a mother myself that Mom raised my sister at a different time in Mom's life. The relationship she had with my sister, I noticed, was more relaxed in many ways. By the time I was out of the house, my sister was just ten years old.

My sister said Mom told her that in the years of my father's imprisonment, *Uncle* was introduced to her at a social event. Mom fell madly in love, but kept their romantic involvement discreet. After my father was killed, Mom and *Uncle* made plans to leave the Philippines together for a new life in a new country.

"He was the love of her life," my sister told me about her father. "They left in a flurry of scandal and gossip. Mom was, after all, the widow of a national hero. She was expected to die a widow."

"Mom's family in China never knew about me," my sister went on, "She had to keep their marriage a secret, so my grandparents never knew I even existed. I think they were married after I was born."

Uncle had played the violin, my sister said, a quality that drew Mom to him in the first place. He pursued a degree in music after we arrived in New York. Mom would ask *Uncle* to supervise my practicing, and occasionally asked me to accompany him at the piano as he played. I still remember finding excuses not to practice when he was home. I look back today to those moments with the same sense of annoyance. *Uncle* liked to show off in front of Mom and criticized my playing and my teachers.

Uncle arrived on a visitor's visa, unlike the immigration status of displaced persons Mom had obtained for herself, my brother, and me. On his visa, *Uncle* could only work at odd jobs like a waiter, and occasional stints as a baby photographer. My sister said the position he had really wanted and which he felt he deserved was that of a concert violinist.

As our lives progressed in the late 1950s and early 1960s, I lived at home and attended college. I heard the frequent and loud verbal battles between Mom and *Uncle*. Mom called him lazy, pointing out the multiple projects he had begun but never completed, and how he never brought in his share of money to support the household. *Uncle* worked nights at the restaurant, so when Mom was at work and we were at school, he slept. When he returned home, I could hear Mom cry about his womanizing, and threatening to leave him if the affairs continued. Mom was always angry and worried about money.

I will never forget how one day in late June, a year or so after we had arrived in New York, Mom told us that we were going to visit the family of a former colleague of my father's. That family had also immigrated to the United States and now lived in Manhattan on Fifth Avenue. Mom rarely made reference to my father or the events that led to his death and our life in America. She had learned a few days before that the Chinese Communist government had allocated funds to surviving members of national heroes, and the widow of the chief of my father's delegation held the details for our family.

School was out for the summer, and Mom took the day off from work. My brother and I wore our best clothes. We took the subway from the Lower East Side to Fifth Avenue. I remember the tall shining glass and steel apartment building. A uniformed man opened the door. Another operated the elevator that took us to the top floor, marked "PH," for penthouse. A western woman, who we later learned was the maid, opened the apartment door and directed us into a sitting room surrounded by mirrors and large plants. Our feet sank into the thick beige carpet as we were shown to the couch where we sat with care and attention. I smelled perfume and *Aunty* appeared.

Mom had already reminded us about our manners and to use the deferential term applied to every adult female. *Aunty* wore an elegant *qipao* and high-heeled shoes. The maid brought us cold drinks and cookies, and *Aunty* remarked how much my brother and I had grown. Mom smiled and spoke with her in formal Chinese, incomprehensible to my brother and me. On the way home that afternoon, I remember how angry Mom looked. My brother and I kept silent. A few months after the meeting, Mom received a check in the mail for $3,000.

"The price for your father's service to country, and your inheritance," she said, just before she slapped the envelope on the kitchen table. "No use talking about it."

She made a down payment on a two-story house in Queens.

"Not their business how I use the money," she said. We moved to the first floor and rented out the second.

Fridays were special. Mom got her weekly paycheck. My brother and I met her at the subway station near the house in Queens with a metal shopping cart to shop for the week's worth of groceries. Many Friday evenings, Mom would sit at the kitchen table, lay aside from her weekly paycheck the money for rent, food, subway tokens; whatever was left, she put in a Christmas club account. My memories of the time before my sister was born did not include *Uncle* in our family scenes. He was usually sleeping in the day when we went out or working at night when we were at home. Mom was able to keep her connection to *Uncle* separate from our lives.

On the months when there was an extra Friday, it meant extra money to celebrate. Mom would take us to our favorite Horn and Hardart automat, where my brother and I giggled at selecting food out of little windows. Afterwards, we would catch a show at the Radio City Music Hall. Mom loved the high-kicking Rockettes, and we, the grandness of it all.

When Mom turned sixty-five, she left *Uncle* in New York and moved to Las Vegas. She would move to California a few years afterwards. My sister had completed college and was out on her own. After Mom left, *Uncle* moved in with the woman with whom he had fathered a child while being married to Mom.

"My time," Mom had said about her move to Las Vegas. She lived on a modest Social Security pension, found a part-time job in a gift shop near The Strip, and indulged in her passion for gambling. I was married, raising a family, and worried about her limited finances.

"What, you forget?" she would say. "I raised you children with nothing. I can take care of myself."

Mom used to send my children different souvenirs from Las Vegas. I've kept the Casino chips and lucky silver dollars encased in plastic and my grandchildren play with them as souvenirs from a great-grandma they never met.

In 1985, five years before she died, I invited Mom to go with me to China for a workshop I was conducting for a group of American teachers and tourists. It was the first time Mom had returned to the country where she was born since leaving it more than forty years before. She was as breathless and excited as a young girl.

"I never thought I would see China again," she said.

We were in Nanjing, her birth city, for a few days. Mom left the tour group to look for her old neighborhood and whatever members of her extended family who might still live there. My grandparents had long since died. Mom came back to the hotel with stories about distant cousins. She learned that my father's remains were excavated from Manila and re- buried in Nanjing along with members of his delegation in the *Tomb of Nine Martyrs,* a site erected two years before our visit by the government of the People's Republic of China to commemorate the 40th anniversary of the men's death. Mom did not want to visit the site.

"Too sad," she said, "Too much *eating bitter.* You go."

Her chest lifted, and she released a quiet sigh. She had raised two children alone, in a strange country, away from the support of parents and family. It was enough. She no longer wanted to be reminded of the losses in her life and the hard times that the Chinese called "*eating bitter.*"

Today, I live in northern California. Recently, during a trip to a nearby casino, I saw several elderly Chinese women get off an excursion bus. One wore a hand-knit hat perched jauntily on her head. She looked so much like Mom that I almost ran to greet her. I called my sister when I got home that day to tell her.

"You've made her St. Ruby," my sister said. "I listened again to that cassette of Mom's voice. After so many years, I had forgotten how annoying her sound."

My sister may be right. Perhaps nostalgia has filtered the memories of the past in the same way brown sepia colors the faces in old photos. But for better or worse, the pull between my mother's life and mine remains as strong as the silk spun by silk worms in the fabric of the jacket she had embroidered for me.

Chasing Memory

"Where are you from?" the taxi driver in Nanjing asked in Mandarin Chinese as he watched me hop into the front passenger seat like a local resident.

"*Meiguo*," I said, making use of the Chinese name for the United States that, in English, I translate as *beautiful country.* "But I was born in Nanjing."

I handed him a business card that I had translated into Chinese. "I'm here with a group of Americans to teach a three-week summer class in English conversation at the University."

I had arrived in Nanjing that July from San Francisco. Nanjing, considered the southern capital of China, is one of the country's earliest established cities, and served as China's capital for a few years before World War II. It is located about 600 miles southeast of Beijing, the northern capital.

"And when did you leave Nanjing?" the driver asked. "You don't speak the Nanjing dialect."

"My family left during the Japanese invasion in World War II. I was just a few weeks old."

"Oh, *huajiao*," he said, applying the term used to describe the Chinese who fled overseas after World War II. "Where did you learn to speak Chinese?"

"From my mother."

"You must be over sixty years old, yes?" he said with a smile. He looked about thirty.

"Good guess," I said. "You know your history."

"My grandparents told me many stories about the war," he said. "It was a difficult time. People suffered a great deal. My grandparents say that we Chinese know how to 'eat bitter' for a better future. Don't you agree?"

It felt strange hearing echoes of the past from a stranger while riding around in a cab in a city I claimed only through the accident of birth. I nodded in response as childhood memories of "eating bitter" tumbled back.

"Never mind what people say, just work hard," my mother used to say. It was her way to mitigate the many disappointments in life. I understood, but the wall of stoicism she built around herself often left me feeling unsupported on the other side.

I felt at ease here, in a country of people with whom I shared a part of history. Yet, I still worried that the language I learned growing up as a New Yorker and a hyphenated Chinese-American might prove inadequate. I heard my voice responding in Chinese and remembered watching my infant son in his crib years ago, staring at his fist with open-mouthed joy. I felt the same astonishment when my childhood Chinese was understood.

I chatted with the cabbie about his life, his wife, and the government's one-child policy.

"It's good for the country. There are too many of us," he said, just before we arrived at the University guest house and he dropped me off.

The next morning, I entered the Oral English classroom where low murmurs greeted me. The

English class was made up of fifteen teachers from the University with careers already tracked into the University system. The teachers looked to be in their late thirties, three of whom were women.

"She's Chinese?" I heard one student whisper in Mandarin.

"Yes, I am," I acknowledged in Chinese, and saw the surprise on their faces. "I was also born here."

"You may be born here, but you're not like us," one of them whispered. It was a common sentiment I heard expressed by many of the Chinese I met in China. The fact that I left China so young meant that my family escaped the bitter experiences their families suffered during the Japanese occupation.

I gave each member of the class an English name and encouraged them to speak in simple sentences. My background became a convenient topic for English conversation. I told them about a workshop I had conducted in China back in 1982.

"My mother came with me," I told them. "She left Nanjing before the war, forty years earlier, and wanted to see the city again."

"Did she look for relatives, Teacher?" one student asked.

"Yes," I said. "My mother found some surviving cousins on my father's side. My father, a diplomat in Nationalist China, was executed in Manila, Philippines, by the Japanese during the war. My mother learned from her relatives that the government had transferred my father's remains to a special tomb in Nanjing. But we didn't have enough time to visit."

"Ah. . . he was a member of the Nationalist government," another student said. I caught the looks some of the students gave each other. Present day China was established in 1949 after a civil war fought between the Nationalist and Communist parties resulted in the overthrow of the Nationalist regime.

"My grandparents told me about the big war with the Japanese," a student said. "It was a dangerous time. The Japanese executed everyone who worked in the Chinese government."

"Our families still talk about that *Great Massacre*," one student explained, referring to what many in America call *The Rape of Nanking.*

"The Japanese slaughtered hundreds of thousands of residents," another student said. "After the war, the Chinese government sent word to families in rural provinces to come re-populate Nanjing. That's when my grandparents settled here in this city."

"Many years ago, a friend sent me a newspaper clipping that described my father's gravesite with an address. My mother had already died," I told the class. "This time, I want to pay my respects."

Most of the students in the class were born during the decades of the '70s and early '80s. They grew up in a time when China had again re-opened its doors to the West. I heard great hope for the future and pride in their stories about themselves and members of their families.

"China has made great progress," another student said. Their national pride was obvious and reminded me of the sentiments my mother shared every time she spoke about her native country.

"You're still Chinese," my mother used to tell me when she saw me too eager to adapt to the habits of an American teenager. "Never mind lipstick and boys. You're not raised like them. Your job is to study and work hard."

The University guest house, built in the '90s, was about a block and half from the main campus classrooms and across the street from a park constructed around the same time. A massive stone sundial situated at the park's entrance occupied a third of the rectangular courtyard space; stone benches and mulberry bushes surrounded the park's outer periphery. At the sundial's base, a poem in Chinese had caught my eye, but my knowledge of written Chinese was insufficient to read it. Instead, I copied down the four lines on a piece of paper to translate later with my Chinese-English dictionary.

The University housed its teachers on the second floor of the guest house, in rooms adjacent to each other. Katie, one of the younger teachers in our group of five American teachers—two of us retired—was on her first trip to China. Her room was next to mine, so we struck up a friendship. A primary school teacher from New York City, Katie, five feet, eleven inches tall, with long blonde hair and a runner's lean frame, told me about her daily running routine.

"I wear my Nike outfit: shirt, running shorts, and shoes," Katie said. "I pull my hair back into a ponytail. Is that ok?"

"Try it," I said, while trying to forewarn her about the impact her appearance might have on the locals. "Nanjing is a cosmopolitan city. But we are not in Chinatown, off the sidewalks of New York."

On weekdays, Katie knocked at my door at 5:30 in the morning, on the way out for her run. It was my cue to head outside to watch a class of about thirty elders in their 60s and 70s, gathered in the open space for tai chi instruction and exercise.

I watched the teacher open the class with a few minutes of review; then he turned on the boom box next to where he stood on a raised platform.

The Chinese music and words flowed out, directing the slow and fluid movements of arms and legs. In some routines, the class used fans, scarves, and wooden sticks in accompaniment to the music.

I liked to sit and listen. Sometimes, I joined the walkers under the trees around the perimeter of the park. Some people swung their arms in gentle motion from back to front, some walked with canes, others stretched by holding onto the stone benches scattered around the park's periphery, and a few people walked backwards, a favorite form of exercise. I caught snatches of different conversations as I walked around. The locals talked about families, recipes, and community events.

After a few days, I recognized familiar faces and noticed how initial looks of curiosity transformed into smiles of recognition and interest. The locals scanned me with their eyes; some spoke to me in Chinese, trying to detect the origin of my accent. But even in a place where I looked more like the people around me, I felt like an outsider.

One morning, Katie ran past me in the park and I gave her a big wave.

"Is that young woman with you?" asked an elderly Chinese man. He was one of the regulars I saw most mornings, usually there before I arrived, and gone by 8:00 a.m. before I left. He carried a baby on his lap whom he kept cool by fanning with a newspaper. His grandson, he told me.

"Yes. She's with our group of American teachers."

"Are you her teacher?"

"No, but I am the oldest person in the group."

"And the only Chinese?" he said, "You must tell them our young people don't show their legs on the street."

He told me he had retired from the University and now lived with his son and daughter-in-law. He talked about his grandson and his pride in the new China.

"This is a different country," he said. "It's good you have returned."

At breakfast, Katie regaled our group with tales of what she had seen during her run: stalls where the local farmers brought produce to sell, food vendors with large pots and pans preparing the daily dishes of dumplings and noodles, and the cages of live poultry that many locals came to buy on site.

"People just gawk at me," Katie said. "It's annoying."

"You look different. You're tall, blonde, with long legs, running in shorts around their neighborhood. So, out of curiosity, they stare. People do that in New York, too," I said.

"I guess I don't notice the stares in New York," Katie said and laughed.

On the last weekend in Nanjing, I made the visit to my father's tomb. The site is located at the southern outskirts of the city in a commemorative park honoring heroes of several wars. I knew many of the signs carried no English translations and invited one of the student guides to come along to read the Chinese.

In the taxi to the park, I showed the female driver photographs my son took of the site during a business trip a few years back. She was one of the few women cabbies I saw around the city. She recognized the place, and during the hour-long ride, asked me the usual questions about where I was from and where I learned to speak Chinese.

"The lessons you learned from your mother stayed with you," she said. "That's good. I can't wait to tell my son. He's just eight years old."

That late July Sunday morning, Nanjing, known as one of the five furnaces of China, lived up to its reputation with humidity and heat reaching almost 100 degrees. The park covered several city blocks, and many families brought their young children to play under the coolness of the trees. My student guide found the park plaques listing the directions to the tomb sites, but no arrows in any direction. We went up and down the same steep stone steps several times and stumbled upon young couples hidden in a few of the park's secluded alcoves.

I was ready to escape from the withering heat for a ride in an air-conditioned taxicab, when my student guide pointed to another route. On a hill near us, I noticed a low building that looked like another guest house.

"I remember reading that the tomb site is near the building which houses the park's caretakers," the student guide said.

We walked towards the building and stepped over a low stone wall. I noticed nine tombstones arranged in a row in a well-tended plot adjacent to the caretaker's building. I approached the nearest one, and recognized the carved Chinese characters that spelled out my father's last name, the inscription, *A Martyr for Country*, and the date of the commemorative plaque, 1983; a year after my mother's visit those many years ago.

The student guide continued down the row of plaques to look at each name. I stood before my father's tomb. His death changed my family's life forever, but the person buried there was a stranger to me. The few details I knew about him came from snippets of information my mother allowed herself to recall. I remembered still the vacant look in her eyes whenever I asked questions about my father.

I tried to remember him. He died before I was five years old. I wanted to honor his memory and leave behind some tangible evidence of my visit. I remembered a small picture I carried in my wallet; the only photograph I have of my parents. I took out the small brown sepia print and squeezed it into a narrow sliver of space between the tomb and the ground.

"Are you ready to leave?" my guide asked. I couldn't answer.

"Look over here." She directed me to face the camera she had brought with her and clicked. "This is why you came."

Back on campus, our group of teachers prepared for the final round of classes, the schedule of student presentations, and the last get-together that concluded the three-week program.

Like the others, I was ready to return home to the United States. In this city of my birth, I felt more American than Chinese

Months later, in my desk drawer, I found the piece of paper on which I had copied the Chinese characters from the sundial in the Nanjing park. I might have lost something in the translation, but in the poet's words about the measure and passage of time, I felt caught between two languages and cultures in a similar way that my passport and driver's license tell two stories about where I'm from.

Noble Gas

I stared at the helium-filled balloons my six and three-year-old grandsons, Ryan and David, directed me to hold. It was a bouquet of their favorite colors, some with pictures of cartoon characters. "Keep the strings tight around your fingers," they said.

The boys were visiting me in California from Boston, where they live with my son and daughter-in-law. I had them to myself for a few hours while their parents shopped. We took the shortcut from my house through the parking lot to the playground. They ran ahead to the jungle gym, climbed on the swings, eventually trying every piece of playground equipment.

A few times, Ryan turned to me, pointed to the balloons with a smile, and mouthed something in my direction. David followed in pantomime.

Sitting on a nearby bench, I felt a cool burst of autumn air tug at the balloon strings. I tightened my hold and thought about the pleasure and pull of family. Helium, I recalled, is the noble gas that heads the series in the periodic table of elements. Weightless, colorless, odorless, and tasteless, it is still able to lift little mylar balls in defiance of gravity. Had the balloons not been tethered to my fingers, I wondered, and smiled at the prospect.

The afternoon brought me back to another fall, decades ago, when my sister Amy and I visited our mother at the Hospice in northern Virginia. Mom loved that time of the year, the fresh air cool enough for a light jacket while leaving her face and hands warmed and exposed to the sun. That morning, Amy and I lowered her into a wheel-chair for a ride around the block. She looked long at the trees in the neighborhood, at the leaves of brilliant reds and orange, and murmured along the way, "Beautiful. . . beautiful."

In the six months since Mom was diag-nosed with cancer, the disease had sucked the physical strength and resilience from her body. She looked frail and was able to stay awake for only a few minutes at a time before falling into deeper and longer stretches of sleep. During the week we were there, the doctor warned that in Mom's state, she could slip into a coma. My brother George was working in Hawaii then, planning to take early retirement in a few years. Even after the diagnosis, he continued to build a house with an in-law apartment for Mom. "She'll come through," he said. I still convinced him to come.

Mom's bed faced the door. She watched George enter the room, and, for an instant, became her former buoyant self. She sat up and flashed a smile. He gave me a questioning look, as if to ask, *Was this trip necessary?*

"She looks fine," he said. He kissed her cheek, held her face in his hands, and examined her "hairdo." The hair was cut close around the face, making her look almost bald from the front.

"Nice, Ma," George said, turning her face for a better look. "So long as you like it, right?" he said.

"My business," she said, her standard response to the countless times in the past comments were made about her individuality.

George's presence always cheered her. I remembered past antics when we were teenagers. At sixteen, George towered above Mom in height. He used to pick her up, swing her around, reduce her to peals of laughter. In the twirl, she overlooked his misdeeds.

"Don't encourage her," Amy said, watching George examine Mom's hair. "She'll want her scissors next to clip the unruly ends."

"What are you talking about," Mom said, and lay her head back. George sat on the other side of her bed and began to take out a few watermelon seeds from the bag he had brought with him. Food, we knew, was a high enjoyment in Mom's life, and watermelon seeds were reminders of an earlier life in China before our family immigrated to this country. Mom used to tell about how she cracked the seeds between her teeth and got so expert that she could hold several of them in her mouth, extract the soft insides one at a time, and spit the empty shells out in sequence. She delighted in seeing the pool of empty shells increase around her place at the table.

Eyes closed, Mom asked George, "What are you eating?" George cracked a few seeds for her and placed the soft insides in her mouth. The salty taste whetted Mom's appetite. She enjoyed the flavor, complained about the blandness of Hospice meals, and longed for the favorite dishes of her youth. Amy went to find the soft ice cream Mom liked. As soon as Amy left, Mom whispered "She's out with her boyfriends, likes to sneak out, you know."

"See? Mom's ok," George said, turning to me.

"Did she tell you I was out cavorting with my boyfriends at the corner candy store?" Amy asked, returning with a dish of soft vanilla swirl. The image of Amy, her middle-aged form fending off the hormonal urges of local youth made the three of us explode into loud laughter. Mom heard the reaction and smiled. Amy fed Mom a few more spoonsful and Mom dozed off. George, dismissing Amy's usual attempt at keeping score between them, re-arranged Mom's pillows, unfolded a newspaper, and suggested that Amy and I take a break.

We returned within an hour to find George flat on the floor in visible pain.

"Mom wanted to go to the bathroom," he said. "I asked if she needed help. She said no. I offered my arm anyway for support and helped her sit up. When she lowered her feet to the floor, her legs gave out."

"So, how did she get back to bed?" Amy asked.

"I lifted her up and carried her back. She couldn't stand on her own. I threw my back out doing it," he said. "The nurse came in, checked on Mom, and gave me some pain medication. I'm down on the floor to relieve the pain. She looked strong. . ."

Mom's breathing was barely audible and we understood the doctor's prediction more clearly. I also knew that regardless of her condition, Mom was aware of George's pain, so I exercised my position as the eldest. "Mom would want you to go home and take care of yourself," I said. George agreed that he needed to leave, despite having spent only half a day with Mom. He inched his way towards her and kissed her cheek. A few hours after George's flight took off, Mom died.

"Grandma, Grandma," I heard my grandsons giggle. "You let one of the balloons go." I was more than a little surprised because I hadn't felt a thing. I gathered the two boys in a hug and watched the little ball lift in noble majesty.

A version of this essay first appeared in *Mom's Literary Magazine*, Fall 2007.

Look-Alike

It wasn't the first time I had driven to meet my friend at the casino near my home. It was on a list of places-to-lunch we had lined up for post-retirement fun. I liked the convenient parking, and my friend, playing the slot machines. The casino, carved out of a hillside in this grape-growing valley of northern California, is visible from the freeway to travelers going in and out of the region. The tent-like structure and the vertical parking units jut out of the landscape in bold defiance.

I was surprised to see a large number of elderly Chinese men and women that day in the casino's main room. They sat among the many rows of slot machines, eyes fixated on the screens, fingers feeding in coins with frenzy. An announcement in Chinese about the day's lucky prizes came over the loudspeaker. It carried me back to the time growing up in a Chinese immigrant family in New York City. My mother used to take me to a supermarket in Chinatown where similar announcements in Chinese were made about that day's specials. Memories jangled around like loose coins in my head.

After lunch, while my friend gambled, I stepped outside and saw a woman waiting for a bus on a bank of benches supplied for tourists. I learned from overhearing a conversation that she came with a group of senior citizens from Oakland's Chinatown, about 75 miles south. The woman looked so much like my mother that I caught myself almost calling out her name.

Mom died over twenty-five years ago. She loved to gamble and used to delight in sitting on a bus during similar excursions, relaxed, and enjoying the scenery. The woman was about Mom's age when she died and looked like how I remembered my mother: hair cropped short and wearing a cloth jacket one size too large, *more for function than fashion*, Mom used to say. She wore the same black walking shoes Mom used to wear, perhaps for the same reason—because the shoes didn't pinch. I wondered if the woman on the bench won any money, or, like Mom, just broke even.

I played with the idea of sitting down next to the woman. I wondered how she would react and what I would say. As I approached the bench, she was digging for something, probably tissues, in a cloth bag that looked handmade. Near her were bundles of used tissues that I guessed went back into the bag once she found what she was looking for, just like Mom's *butterflies*, as she called them. They flew in and out every time she looked in the bag for something. *Why throw them away?* she used to say. *Some, I use again.*

Mom carried a similar kind of bag, made from large squares of colorful remnants she found in fabric stores. She sewed three sides of the square together like a pocket and added a drawstring to pull the sides shut. *See, my bag,* Mom used to say, proud of her thrift and ingenuity.

I sat down on the bench, my arm brushing the sleeve of the woman's jacket. She turned and looked at me, annoyed. *She's probably wondering why I chose to sit on this bench when there are other benches available*, I thought. I gave a small smile and assumed she spoke little English, only the Cantonese dialect of many Chinese in Chinatown. It was not a dialect my family spoke, but I knew a few words. "How are you?" I said, hoping that my accent sounded familiar enough to calm her about my presence. She looked from me to the bag, shook her head, and mumbled something that I understood as "Crazy person..."

There on the bench, I felt as if I were sitting next to my mother. My body stayed bolted to the seat as thoughts swirled around in my head.

I've been holding on to this story for over sixty years. I've stopped counting the number of times I wanted to tell you, but I knew you'd never believe me. You did the best you could and life was hard. But the man you told us to call "Uncle" abused me. I was just twelve years old. I wanted to run away. On the nights you thought I was talking in my sleep, he was there. I wanted you to come into my room. Instead, you called him to check on me.

The woman found what she was digging for, took a steamed bun out of her bag and began to eat, oblivious to my dilemma. She took a few sips of tea from a thermos she produced from the same bag. A friend of hers soon appeared. She tapped the woman's arm and asked in their dialect, assuming I didn't understand, "Is this someone you know?" The mother look-alike shook her head. Her friend mumbled, "Is she crazy?" and shot me a look my mother used to call "snake eyes."

I didn't move, my mind still whirling. *I tried to stop the abuse. I wore a bra, shirt, belt, and jeans to bed every night. I tried not to be home when you were working. I stayed late at school, went to the library or to my girlfriend's house. I tried to be a dutiful daughter and not make you worry. You stopped trusting him after you discovered he went back to cheating with other women, but it was too late by then.*

At that moment, the newcomer squeezed herself between me and the mother-look-alike. The two women turned away from me and began a conversation. They talked about the panoramic view before them, the town below, and the vista of rolling hills on the horizon. I felt a strange dryness in my throat and wondered if I had spoken my thoughts out loud. I saw the bus winding its way up the steep grade to the casino parking lot, and heard the announcement over the loudspeaker in Chinese and English: "The Oakland bus is here. All passengers line up outside."

The mother-look-alike began to cry. Her friend tried to calm her, and helped to collect her *butterfly* tissues back into the bag. To my surprise, the look-alike leaned back on the bench, turned towards me to motion that she had to go. I wished I knew enough words in her dialect to ask why she was crying. I wanted to believe that she understood how I felt. Other passengers began to drift out of the casino, and a bus line began to form. I left the bench, somewhat disoriented, and walked away.

"Hey, wait up," my friend called out, running after me, "I thought you had left. Were you playing the machines?"

"No," I said, "I saw a woman who reminded me of my mother."

"Did you talk to her?"

"Yes, I think I did. I told her stuff I had wanted to tell my mother, stuff that I've been carrying around for a while."

"But she's a total stranger…what kind of stuff did you unload?"

"Personal crap."

"What are you, crazy?"

"She didn't feel like a stranger."

"Did you think she was a holographic image projected from the beyond? But look," my friend said, turning back to the bus, "those two women seem to be waving at us. Let's wave back."

Reading the Panels on Trucks

"Ryan, look, see the Chinese words on that truck panel?" I asked my then seven-year-old grandson as we drove south from my home in Sonoma County to the San Francisco waterfront.

My son and his family were making their annual visit from back east and had rented a minivan for the week. That morning I was sandwiched in the second row, flanked on both sides by Ryan and his five-year-old brother, David, snug in their car seats, while my son drove and my daughter-in-law sat up front. We passed many trucks along the way transporting goods to and from the ports of Oakland and San Francisco. Some of the trucks had side panels with words in different languages. I had told the family I was again learning to read Chinese.

"What does the truck say?" Ryan asked.

"*China Import and Export Company,*" I said.

"No, Grandma, not the English. Read the Chinese words."

"China, *Something, Something, Something,* Company," I said, recognizing only four of the ten Chinese characters printed on that panel.

Ryan giggled, leaned over to his brother and said, "Hey, David, Grandma said, the '*Something, Something, Something* Company.'"

"What grade are you in Chinese class, Grandma?" David asked.

"I'm not in a class. I'm taking private lessons with a teacher."

"Why? Are you too old to be in school?"

"It's different because I already speak Chinese."

"Mom and Dad," Ryan yelled to his parents, "Grandma is trying to read the Chinese on the truck!"

"That should keep Grandma busy," my son answered from the front seat.

I explained to my grandsons that I needed to recognize 900 Chinese characters to read simple books and 4,000 characters to read a newspaper.

"How many do you need to read a truck, Grandma?" David asked.

My mind went back to the early 1950s with my mother, a young widow who had immigrated with my brother and me to New York City and safeguarded us from the harsh consequences of World War II in China. Back then, my mother began teaching me to read and write Chinese before her days became consumed with meeting the demands of working and adjusting to a new life. She expected me to continue to learn the language of my culture.

"Don't forget, "she said. "It's your mother tongue."

Decades later, I can still converse in Chinese, but recognize only a few written characters, in part because I had learned the earlier and more complex method of Chinese writing. After 1956, the Chinese Communist government modified the traditional written Chinese calligraphy into a simpler way to read and write in Chinese. In the process, each Chinese character became associated with

Pinyin, translated as "spell sound;" the sound of each Chinese character, spelled in English. *Pinyin* became the method for learning and teaching Chinese phonetically to English-speaking peoples.

I still spoke and understood spoken Chinese but the few written characters I remembered from childhood appeared less recognizable in the *Pinyin* method.

Starting as a young girl, English became my dominant language; it provided the key to the future, the language to learn in order to belong and to associate with classmates. Mom understood this was also true in her situation. English soon replaced Chinese as the spoken language at home.

Outside the van window, I noticed the traffic had become more congested and felt a tug at my right arm.

"Grandma, I'm learning to read, too," David said. "You can come to pre-school with me." I gave him a hug.

"Can you read the Chinese on *that* truck, Grandma?" he said.

"Well, let's see," I said. "The panel on that truck says, *Shanghai Chinese Restaurant.*" Then I read it in Chinese.

"Yes!" my grandsons yelled and gestured with their thumbs up in the air. "Mom and Dad, Grandma read the Chinese on the truck panel!"

Two years later, my husband and I were considering relocating to New England. Before going back east to look at condominium properties, I spent a weekend with my son and grandsons before they left California. The boys were growing up, becoming more independent and developing clear and distinct personalities.

I was in the kitchen preparing to serve dinner when David who had just turned seven, came in from the TV room to keep me company.

"I've had a hard life, you know, Grandma," he said.

"Oh, why do you say that?" I asked.

"I had an operation when I was a baby, my uncle died, and my parents divorced," he said.

My heart leapt to my throat. I could barely answer. I remembered each of the events my grandson referred to. When he was an infant, he did undergo corrective surgery for a case of undescended testicles. The procedure went well and aside from a few months of discomfort, we were all thrilled to see him once again thrive. His favorite uncle, his mother's brother, died by suicide the year before, and the family was still recovering from the shock. A few months after the tragedy, my son and his wife had decided to separate.

"I know," I told my grandson, and quickly gave him a hug. "But the operation you had went fine. I know it was sad about Uncle Chris, but you have good memories, right? And your mom and dad are still your mom and dad. They love you very much; you know that, don't you?"

He nodded.

"And you and your brother are adjusting, right?" I said.

"Hm…mm." He left the kitchen.

I was struck by my grandson's wisdom. Life had been hard. I remembered how surprised and sad I felt at the time of my son's impending divorce. I didn't know what to say except to hug my grandsons, tighter.

During the intervening months, I watched my son, my youngest, balance the pressures of being a single dad and the work in his job as chief of a corporate legal team. I knew he would not ask that we relocate back to the area just for him. Yet, as his mother, I knew he needed the support of family. His father had wanted to offer immediate assistance, but I waited, which is partly why the decision to return felt so comfortable. I began to look forward to moving back to Boston and its many diversions, to be closer to family and long-time friends, and to reclaim part of the person I thought I was.

I have reached an age when I can better manage the uncertainties of life. Like the once-congested lanes of traffic on our trip that day, the anxiety and confusion I sometimes feel for my children and grandchildren will similarly clear. In the meantime, I'm still trying to learn Chinese and look for every opportunity along the way to practice.

Duty-Free Zone

"I'll bank it for the next time," said my nine-year-old grandson, Ryan. We were shopping with his seven-year-old brother, David, during one of my regular visits to Massachusetts. Since I lived in California, the distance was too far for me to attend all their birthday parties, school events, and holidays in person. Eventually, I proposed that in lieu of mailing cards and gifts, I'd take the boys to the local toy stores whenever I visited. They happily accepted the alternative.

The first stop we made that day was at a local branch of a national chain. There I watched Ryan consider the wide variety and selection of toys, the shelves of electronic games, motorized models, and mechanical sets. When he walked towards the book section and took several books off the shelf to browse, I noticed he was taller than the last time I saw him. His personality seemed to be a combination of my own two sons—his father and his uncle— articulate like his father, quiet and reflective like his uncle,

His brother, David, was a head shorter, his features taken more from his mother's side. An extrovert, he was as chatty as his father was at his age. He followed Ryan around the store, liked every toy he touched, but watched and waited for his brother to make a choice. After Ryan announced his decision to bank his purchase, David held on to the twin motorized plastic motorcycles he had started carrying two aisles earlier.

"I'd like to buy this, Grandma," he said with a huge smile on his face.

Back in the car and firmly strapped into the backseat, the boys bantered with each other, arguing over the direction I should take to get out of the parking lot. I liked listening to their conversation and remembered how my sons behaved in similar ways so many years ago. Fortunately, only memories of brotherly exchange and camaraderie remain with me today.

I thought how lucky my grandsons were to have parents who understood the significance of choices and encouraged the ability to make them. I hoped my grandsons would learn to grow in the habit. During my childhood, children did as they were told and accepted without question what parents decided for them. I remembered the dutiful periods of accommodation in my youth, the number of times I had to wait until I got old enough to wear makeup, date boys, and years later, when I was finally able to finish my education, establish a career and start a family. To make waiting easier during the early years, I used to imagine my mother wrapping me in a cloak of high expectations. At a time, which she chose, she would let me emerge, and I would instantly know how to act grown up.

Due to my mother's influence, from the time she, my brother, and I arrived in the United States as immigrants from China in 1948, my life focused on little else except practicing the piano and performing concerts. With marriage and the birth of my sons in the mid-to-late 1960s, my attention turned towards children and home.

It would be another twenty-five years, after my sons had completed college and my husband had retired from his University faculty position in 1990, that I felt sufficiently duty-free to pursue a position in another town. I left the administrative position I had held at Emmanuel College in Boston for more than twenty-five years and accepted a different position at California State University, Humboldt, in northern California.

In 1992, My husband and I relocated and lived in California. Ten years later, I retired from the administrative position that first drew me to the state. Around the same time, in Massachusetts, my first grandson was born, and a few years later, the second. I felt the tug to move back east, to be closer to a city and to experience a life free from former responsibilities.

Not long before my husband and I decided to leave California, I received a phone call from my much younger sister who lives in Washington, D.C. Fifteen years younger, we shared the same mother, but my sister's father was Mom's second husband, whom she married when I was 14 years old. She wanted to tell me about a concert she had attended the night before.

"Don't you miss the excitement of performing?" my sister asked. "The pianist showed such control and mastery. You must miss it."

"Who was the pianist?"

"A young guy. A Juilliard graduate, like you."

"And what did he play?" I asked, ready to guess that he had chosen a program of crowd pleasers.

"Some Mozart, and fabulous Chopin and Liszt pieces," she said. "Great technique. And oh, for encore he played that piece you used to, I forgot the name. But the audience loved it. When I was little, I loved going to your concerts. It was exciting to see you on stage. Mom and I were so proud. Do you still play?"

"I haven't played in years," I said. "In fact, I've been thinking about giving away the piano the next time I move anywhere."

"Can I have it?" she asked.

My sister's question surprised me. I knew she always had an attachment to my piano, but her request stirred in me a sense of yearning I thought had been extinguished long ago. I thought the drive to perform, an ambition burnished from decades spent practicing and planning concerts, had loosened its grip, but I carried the piano with me everywhere I moved, less like a lucky charm than a remembrance of the past. For a great part of my life growing up and into adulthood, the piano was the single reason my mother had given me for having immigrated to the United States.

"We came to this country because of your talent," she had said.

I held back a response to my sister's request. *I'm not ready to give the piano away*, I thought. *Not yet.*

"Think about it, ok?" she repeated.

As an eleven-year-old, I dutifully attended the Juilliard Preparatory Division—the Prep, as it was known in the early 1950s. The school was in uptown Manhattan. Years later, it would move to its present mid-town Lincoln Center location. The Prep accepted students from primary and secondary grades across the country and internationally. A young foreigner myself, I met students who had been sent on their own from faraway countries, like Israel, to attend the school. Many lived with relatives they had just met. The talents of the students were of such high caliber that at the tender ages of seven, eight, and nine, many were already world-class concert artists. There was a rarified atmosphere at the school, an environment made for intense competition and hard work. I think often of those days with a mixture of pride and fear; every act of accomplishment meant having persevered through the intense and hurtful exercise of criticism and competition.

Unlike my grandsons, who were driven to school, lessons, and events, as a student at the Prep, I took the subway every Saturday from where we lived in Queens to Manhattan. I spent the day in a schedule of private piano lessons, music theory, and ensemble classes. My mother, occupied with the daily struggles of supporting the family, expected me to manage by myself. She taught me how to navigate the subway system. I didn't have a choice and didn't want to cause her additional worries.

It was the late '50s and early '60s, tumultuous times: the assassination of President Kennedy and the Freedom March culminating with Martin Luther King Jr.'s "I Have a Dream" speech. The publication of Betty Friedan's *The Feminine Mystique* opened up worlds of possibilities.

I used to hear Mom yell, "That's right!" at TV news broadcasts when issues were being fought over by different women's groups. Mom valued independence and the freedom of choice for women, but it was different for me, her daughter. She made sure I understood about "saving face" and "staying Chinese."

"You have to work harder. You're Chinese," she reminded me. "Doesn't matter how long you live in this country. You're still an outsider."

Almost daily, there were situations Mom pointed to where she expected me to acquiesce with quiet dignity. To do otherwise, I knew, would reflect badly on her, our immediate family, and other Chinese.

After completing high school, I was accepted into the college division at Juilliard, and after graduation, I received a Fulbright grant for graduate study in Paris, France. I jumped at the chance to study abroad; I knew it would be the only excuse Mom would accept for me to leave home. I spent a year in Paris, learning French, studying piano at the Paris Conservatory, and trying to imagine myself living separate from my family.

"I was surprised that Mom let you move to Boston when you returned," my sister had said.

Sometime during the year I located to Boston, I met my husband at a dinner party thrown by mutual friends. From the start, I knew my mother approved. He was Chinese, educated, and had a future. My husband and I married within the year of our meeting, and we settled in Massachusetts, where he held a teaching position. I performed still, but soon, with two young boys, I found a teaching position that gave me the flexibility to manage work and family. After our sons were grown, my career took me and my husband to California, which we both enjoyed, until it was time to be directed by a new set of duties.

I still remember the morning I opened an email from a longtime friend, Judy. She and I became friends as fourteen-year-old students at the Juilliard Prep, and have remained friends through the years.

"Are you still planning to move back to New York like you promised yourself?" she wrote. "It's been a while since you retired, right?"

"New York may have to wait," I replied. "Boston seems more realistic. The grandkids are there."

"What about Lover Boy?" she asked, calling my husband by the nickname given to him forty years ago by her and other friends after they discovered our seventeen-year difference in age. "What's his preference?"

"It's hard to know what he wants," I said.

I thought about a similar time in my mother's life; when her kids were grown, she left her husband in New York and moved to Las Vegas.

"My time," my mother had said.

"And you know, it doesn't really matter, "I told Judy. "It's my time."

Sparks

I wrote about my mother's indomitable spirit and abundant resilience in the first edition, and how in 1990, she died at the age of seventy-six. Now, at eighty-two, I am older than my mother was when she died. I often wonder how she might have looked or felt at my age.

Mom used to say, "No matter how good your English, or how smart you are, you will always look different."

A few years ago, I was on the bus from Framingham, a suburb of Boston, going to New York to spend a weekend with my old friend from high school. We had plans to see a Broadway show, have dinner, and celebrate our lives as eighty-year-old grandmothers.

Like most weekends, the bus to New York was crowded. I discovered an empty seat and prepared to settle down with a book.

"Where are you from?" the woman asked as she settled herself next to me.

"New York," I said, the standard answer for someone who grew up, like I did, in New York City. I smiled.

"No, I mean, where are you really from?" the woman asked again.

"New York City," I said. This time I merely smiled politely and looked down at my book to avoid her gaze and the all-too-familiar questions I knew could follow.

Out of the corner of my eye, I saw "that look" on her face. The woman, probably my age, was dressed in what my teen-age friends and I used to describe as "Junior League": matching jacket and slacks, pearl earrings, and sensible pumps. She glanced at my sweatpants, old sweater, and looked away.

"You see? I told you," I heard my mother's voice, and became the eleven-year-old Chinese immigrant girl growing up in New York's Lower East Side.

"This is silly," I told myself, as my mind raced back to the place I lived for my most formative years.

I was in the seventh grade at the local Catholic school and my classmates came from Irish and Italian immigrant families. I wanted to fit in and be like them. They had last names Sister could pronounce. Often, when Sister called on them in class, she used "Miss" or "Mister" with their last names. I was the only one she always called by my first name because she said my last name, Siao, was unpronounceable. I remember still the way my classmates looked at me when she said that.

My mother had recently moved us from a large, single basement room to a walk-up apartment on the fourth floor of an old tenement building. It was luxurious compared to the basement room. The apartment had a kitchen that doubled as a dining room, a living room with an upright piano (among the reasons why my mother chose the apartment), and two separate narrow alcoves that functioned as sleeping areas. My mother had one with *Uncle,* and my brother and I shared the other, our beds aligned in a straight line.

The buildings in the rundown neighborhood were built close together. When I walked up and down the stairs, I could see into the Jewish synagogue in the building next door. On Fridays, I often saw men in long dark coats, heads bowed, praying and rocking, and heard the low rumble of prayers. And sometimes, I watched women, children, and families come to celebrate the Sabbath.

At school, Sister told stories about her family from Ireland, about the country and its customs. Each day, she asked a different classmate to talk about their family. As the only student without an Irish or Italian last name, I was rarely called on to tell my story.

One day, Sister announced that the class was going to produce a St. Patrick's Day show. Sister would teach the girls to tap dance to popular Irish songs and the boys were assigned different activities. Sister told me that I was to join the tap dance group with the other girls.

I was thrilled. We practiced and practiced, every dance step, every shuffle and kick Sister taught us. We rehearsed late afternoons and evenings. Sister tested our memorization daily to make sure we learned the words to the songs, "When Irish Eyes are Smiling" and "McNamara's Band."

My mother said, "Why not ask to play the piano?"

"The teacher wanted another teacher to play," I said. My mother accepted the explanation. I told her Sister wanted us to buy metal taps for our shoes.

My mother shook her head, looked slightly annoyed, but took my shoes the next day to the neighborhood shoe repair shop to get the metal taps attached. After she brought the shoes home, I clicked and shuffled my feet in them and loved the sounds the metal taps made. I remember how happy I felt wearing green outfits like everyone else to celebrate the day.

On yet another day, Sister told us that each student would participate in confirmation ceremonies the following Sunday. She gave no other explanation. Sunday arrived. I knelt by the altar, waiting my turn, and felt Sister's strong hand on my shoulder.

"Are you baptized, dear?" she asked.

"I don't know," I said.

Sister promptly took me out of the line, brought me before the priest who baptized me on the spot, and put me back into the confirmation line. I came home and told my mother what happened.

"Never mind," my mother said. "You did as you were told."

My mother was not Catholic, but she loved churches and houses of worship, even though she rarely attended services. She sent my brother and me to parochial schools for the discipline and quality of the education. Going to church was something my brother and I did on Sundays. Rarely did I hear my mother speak of herself as a participant in any ceremony or as a member in any church or temple. She described my grandmother as a devout Buddhist. My brother became an altar boy after he was confirmed.

"God is God," my mother said. "God is everywhere, in churches, synagogues, everywhere."

The jolting bus shook me free of those long-ago memories and I looked out the window. I saw the greener scenes of the smaller western Massachusetts towns recede. Along the Massachusetts Turnpike, the taller buildings of Connecticut and tighter neighborhoods came into view. Soon, more tall buildings emerged with bold advertisements for storage, insurance, and politicians painted on their sides. I knew we were getting closer, and before long, the exits on the New York Thruway showed the more familiar names: Bruckner Boulevard, Whitestone Bridge, and 155th Street. My spirit lifted in anticipation of the numbered streets of Manhattan as the bus passed local landmarks along Fifth Avenue: the Guggenheim Museum, the Metropolitan Museum of Art, Central Park, the Rockefeller skating rink, and St. Patrick's Cathedral.

The values my mother passed on to my brother and me, hard work, generosity, and kindness, were not anchored to any religion or church, but set within the context of Chinese culture, tradition, and history. As a parent, I watched my mother's toughness soften with my sons, her grandchildren. And there were the times growing up when I heard her sing, in Chinese, the first line of the Christian hymn, *Jesus loves me, this I know,* quietly to herself. I saw tears in her eyes during those moments, but as soon as she felt my gaze, she turned her face away.

I remembered one day, decades ago, my brother and I came home from school to proclaim at dinner, "Sister told us, no meat on Fridays."

My mother said, "Ok," and cleared away the meat dishes she had prepared for that evening's meal.

As she cleared the table, she looked at us and asked, "Do you really think God cares if you eat meat on Fridays?"

That long bus ride to New York City also sparked memories of silly and elusive dreams, like my childhood wish to learn to swim.

Decades ago, when I brought my young sons to our local YMCA for their swimming lessons, I signed up for an adult beginner group class.

Learning the first steps, putting my face in the water, feeling the confidence of being buoyed by the water, I managed to float and swim from one short side of the pool to the other. I was proud of myself.

Many years later, I tried again, with an individual brush-up lesson. I was assigned to an instructor who was too young to understand how fear of the water manifested itself in adults. She chatted with a colleague while holding my head under water. Panicked, I bolted up, sputtered an excuse, and left the pool. So much for that dream.

As the bus wended its way in and out of the New York City streets, I saw sidewalks crowded with people, a field of yellow taxicabs skirting in and out between cars and buses, and a few pedicabs maneuvering around the traffic with more frenzy and daring. Even after many decades spent away from the City, the frenetic energy of New York was pulling me back. I was not born here and have lived most of my life in Massachusetts with almost two decades in California, but if I am from anywhere, it's New York, the place my mother brought me, the place that made me. It has always felt most like home.

The bus arrived at its final stop. I looked around, gathered my belongings, relieved to see my seatmate stepping off the bus. I had no need to explain.

Coming to Age

In 1990, my husband Gilbert retired at seventy years old, the same year my mother died at age seventy-six. He was Professor Emeritus from the Worcester Polytechnic Institute in Massachusetts, an institution he loved and where he devoted over forty years to teaching students and conducting research.

His retirement gave me the opportunity to pursue professional positions out of state, and in 1992, I accepted an administrative position at Humboldt State University, Arcata, California, the northernmost campus of the California State University system. California attracted me because of its student diversity and the chance to work in a large public university system. The campus is located in an area of physical beauty behind the giant redwood trees the locals refer to as the Redwood Curtain. We found a house to rent near the campus, in a culture and environment different from the urban surroundings I knew and in which I grew up.

We arrived in the fall, at the beginning of the academic year, towards the end of the peak rhododendron season. During the spring, people came from different parts of the state to admire the brilliant bursts of scarlet, pink, purple, and white blossoms of the "rhodies." There were still the beautiful blooms left on the bushes in the backyard of the house we rented. Damp from the morning dew, the flowers shimmered in brilliant color under the sun.

I began in a new position with its familiar administrative challenges. The campus, near several Native American tribes, created environments that allowed me to learn and work with many Native American students, staff, and programs. I learned about the culture and history of the students and their families. To this day, those experiences remain the highlight of my time in California.

As I adjusted to the new responsibilities and surroundings, I watched Gilbert slowly shift his attention away from the formal world of academics he left behind. He took lessons to improve his ukulele playing, enrolled in classes on wood carving, and turned the living room into a workshop. After forty years of living, working, and raising a family in New England, we adjusted to the move and began to settle into our new lives.

In 2000, after Gilbert turned eighty, I felt with greater urgency the reality of the age gap between us. I wrote previously about our seventeen-year age difference and how I had assumed the major tasks and responsibilities for childrearing and family. Now, I asked myself, *what-if* I died before him while we were still in California? *What-next* steps should I take to ensure he was taken care of? Had I thought of everything?

I knew I could not leave him alone in California, far away from family and the familiar environment of New England. My sons, immersed in their own lives, were aware of my concerns. Within a few years, I decided to retire from my university position, and in 2011, after eighteen years in California, we returned to New England.

We moved into a condominium in Cambridge, a neighborhood my husband knew, near the bookstores and college environment he loved.

In personality and temperament, Gilbert was a private person, a man of few words. He preferred the solitude of reading and study to social gatherings, except those with family and old friends. A couple of years after moving back to Cambridge, I began to notice a gradual decline in Gilbert's physical and mental capacities. We coped with the situation for a while, but soon, the family realized that assisted living was a safer option. Gilbert moved into St. Patrick's Manor in Framingham, along with his ukulele and his favorite African Djembe drum.

Each day I visited him, I watched with surprise how well and comfortably he adapted to the routine and schedule. Best of all, I watched him lead a group sing-along with his ukulele. He learned to play several different drums, including a metal Middle Eastern hand drum and bongos. I saw him turn his focus away from the ukulele after several incidents in which he could not remember where to place his fingers for the chords. On many days, the joy and satisfaction from playing the instruments reflected on his face. I watched my husband allow himself the time and space to connect to his love of music, to make music, and to experience a youthful curiosity. Gilbert died in 2018, two months before his ninety-eighth birthday.

"He had a good life," Mom's voice often reminds me. Since she died, my conversations with her are better than any I remember having with her during the years she was alive. "He lived to see the birth of all three grandsons, and his sons doing well. You took good care of him. That's a good life."

I remember telling my sister who lives in Northern Virginia about the conversations.

"How often are you having these conversations?" my sister replied. "By the way, did you ever notice how annoying Mom's voice can get after listening for a while?" We laughed.

A two-foot-high stone Buddha sits at the entry to my Cambridge apartment. I brought it with me when we moved from California. After Gilbert died, I placed the striped wool cap he wore every day on the statue's bald head and tucked a small six-inch stuffed black and white panda, dressed in a red Harvard vest, in the crook of the statue's arms that hold the globe. Gilbert had carried the little panda on his walker during his travels around the halls of the nursing home. The staff waved and called him, affectionately, the Professor.

My two adult sons, Kevin, from California, and Colin, from Vermont, have stopped in for a visit. I've kept them up to date about my "cosmic" conversations.

"Still talking to Grandma? What's the latest?" one of them asks.

"Has Dad joined in?" from the other.

"You know Dad," I remind them. "He was never much of a talker. He listened and laughed."

As my sons banter and tease me, I look over at the stone Buddha.

"Remember Dad's panda?" I ask.

"Of course. He tied it to his walker during his walks around the halls."

"He loved that little panda," Kevin says.

"The staff used to wave back at him and call him 'Professor!'" Colin chimes in.

"I remember Dad used to tell us about Buddha's long earlobes."

"Long life and wisdom, Dad used to say."

"So, Mom, there are now four of you in these conversations, correct? Grandma, Dad, and Uncle George."

"Don't mock," I say.

"Just teasing, trying to keep track."

Uncle George. The mention of my brother's name floods me with feelings of sadness and nostalgia. After he retired from a career in the FBI, he and his family settled in Arizona. In 2012, a year after our return from California, my brother died from cancer at the age of seventy-one. With his death, I lost the one person with whom I shared a common past.

In the faded family photographs my sister-in-law keeps, I see one taken when my brother and I were around the ages of eleven and eight. We jumped up and down, clowned around on the upper deck of the ship that brought us from the Philippines to New York. Then there's that photo of him around age ten with a happy grin on his face posing next to a toy machine gun, a Christmas present, in a living room from the past.

"You remember the letter you wrote the boys when you turned sixty-five?" my brother's voice joins the teasing. "Your last will and testament?"

I smile. While we were still in California, I recognized the need to provide guidance for my sons should I die before Gilbert. I called my brother to ask him if he was willing to be named in the will. He had agreed with a laugh.

In coming to age, I look back and recognize the forces of history, culture, and geography that shaped my life in similar ways to that of my mother's. The other consequences to age, such as the body's delayed reaction and accommodations to the ordinary activities of walking, running, or playing with grandsons, have become ordinary. I find comfort, understanding and acceptance residing in the layers of time between the past and present.

Nowadays

It is late summer, 2020, the year our lives divided into "before" or "during" the Covid-19 pandemic. Being able to go see a movie as the mood strikes, plan a weekend of theatre fun in New York, or just call friends for lunch on a whim are among the spontaneous pleasures that are on temporary hold. However, I am still able to take my usual morning walk around the grounds of Mount Auburn Cemetery, Cambridge, a national historic landmark known for its colonial history, charming landscaping, and natural environment. I choose the quieter paths to walk with comfort and ease. Along the way, I pass the stone marker where my husband Gilbert's name is etched and where we buried his ashes in 2018.

A new circular garden has been completed since his death. I sit on one of the benches and watch the outdoor fountain spurt its sprays. Around the circle, I see dots of lavender and yellow flowers, red berry bushes nestled carefully among the tall grasses, and busy bees engaged in their tasks. The place calls up voices and spirits of the past.

This morning, a butterfly flies by with its wings of orange and black. It alights on a flower, wings outspread, completely still, drunk with the flower's nectar. In my head, I hear my husband's voice, "Take care of yourself, ok?" I nod and smile in remembrance.

Nowadays, I miss not being able to see any family members in person, even though the weekly Zoom calls compensate somewhat for the loss. Each Sunday, I get online and wait eagerly to see my sons and grandsons. I listen as they take turns talking about their lives. The enthusiasm, connections, and camaraderie I take away from their conversations sustain me from week to week.

I delight in watching my grandsons grow and step fully into their own lives. I watch them learn from experience, filled with curiosity and kindness as they develop into young men of quality and integrity.

I see Gilbert reflected in the character and temperament of my two sons, confident that their father still smiles in pride and approval. My abundant joy in them, envelopes my daughters-in-law, the mothers of my grandsons. Together, the families reflect the grace, generosity, and resilience of past generations.

I think back often to the primary role music played in my arrival to the United States and how it shaped my professional life after graduating from the Juilliard School. Today, I mourn the losses unleashed by the pandemic upon the health and sustainability of the performing arts, individual artists, and arts groups. The vulnerability of concert halls, museums, theaters, and the variety of performing venues, as well as the sacrifices borne by individual musicians, writers, and performers are immeasurable. At the same time, I marvel at the daily emergence of new and different formats for artistic expression, creation, and invention in the various mediums of video and audio technology. I look to them to restore energy, hope, and meaning to life.

In my later years, I began to explore the music of language and the art of writing. Words have helped me express my awe of family, of belonging, and of a strong connection to place. My stories and memories flow in the same waters as that of past generations, guided by the strong currents of love and gratitude. Aided by its own rhythms, and momentum, my writing seeks its own path and place.

Photo Gallery

Lily, Colin, Kevin, Gilbert (1988)

Gilbert (2013)

Gilbert playing ukelele (2016)

Ryan, Colin, David, Kevin (2018)

Colin Owyang (2018)

Kevin Owyang (2020)

Colin, David, Connor, Ryan (2019)

Ryan, David, and Mom, Emmeline (2018)

Colin, and sons (2018)

Connor and Mom, Deirdre (2019)

Connor (2020)

Above: George, Ruth, daughters, Christina, Aline (1993)
Below: George, Ruth (2007)

George and Lily (2004)

Amy (2020)

Mom, Lily, Amy (1961)

About the Author

Lily Siao Owyang, given the birthname, *Xiao Lu Sheng,* was born in July, 1937, in Nanjing, China, the same month, year, and place as the Luguo Jiao Bridge Incident, when Japan declared war on China at the start of World War II. Her Chinese name, *Lu Sheng*, literally translates as "Born at the time of the Luguo Jiao Bridge Incident"; yet, growing up, her mother rarely spoke of the choice or the significance to her.

Within weeks of her birth, her father, a diplomat in the Chinese Nationalist Government, fled with his wife and infant daughter from the chaos of war and re-located to Manila, Philippines. There, during the war, her father was captured by the Japanese government and executed along with other diplomat colleagues.

In 1948, eleven-year-old Lily, her mother, and eight-year-old brother emigrated to the United States so Lily could attend the Juilliard School of Music in New York. After graduating from Juilliard, she embarked on a performing career as a concert pianist.

In 1965, she married Gilbert Owyang, a college professor, and soon, with two young sons to raise, her career focused more on teaching than concertizing. She completed her doctorate degree, contributed to concert reviews as a music critic for a metropolitan newspaper, and moved into college administration in institutions in New England and California, where she remained until she retired in 2000.

After her mother's death in 1990, she turned to writing to understand how the early influences in her life contributed and shaped her later years. This led to the publication of the first edition of her essays in 2010. In 2011, she and Gilbert returned from California to the Boston area to be closer to family and friends. In 2018, after Gilbert died, she began the later essays to this second edition.

Acknowledgements

As a young Chinese immigrant child growing up in Lower East Side, New York, I never thought writing was a path for me to explore. Back then, the English language was new and belonged to parts of the world that felt separate from me.

But words always fascinated me. They belonged to the world of books, films, and conversations. At grammar school, I learned about homonyms, synonyms, and antonyms. I liked the sounds and the way words caught my tongue. During high school and the years following, I began to understand how words gave me tools to find meaning in new surroundings along with my place in them.

As an adult, I participated in different writing workshops to learn the craft of writing. I learned the satisfaction and exhilaration of a good sentence. Today, I continue to rely upon the wisdom of writers and their work in several mediums.

I've had many wonderful guides and supporters over the years, but in the second edition of this collection, I owe continued thanks and deep gratitude to the counsel, insight, and generosity of one of my early mentors, Susan Bono, editor, and valued friend.

To the wonderful and loyal friends with whom I grew up, and to the many I made during recent decades: your friendship sustains and nourishes my spirit. The lessons I have learned from our conversations support and guide me with steadiness and courage.

To my sons and grandsons, Kevin, Colin, Ryan, David, and Connor: your presence and love reflect the devotion and legacy of your late father and grandfather and bring rich meaning to my life as mother and grandmother. To the other members of my beloved family-sister, Amy, sister-in-law Ruth, nieces, Aline and Christina, my daughters-in-law, Emmeline, and Deirdre, as well as to members of their extended family, I share the satisfaction of completing this project and claim for myself any mistakes or regrets in this second edition's timeline or narrative.

And in loving memory, I celebrate Gilbert, George, and Mom.

Made in the USA
Middletown, DE
19 August 2022

71747886R00066